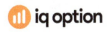

OPTIONS TRADING

FOR

BEGINNERS

A complete step by step guide to Create Your Investment Strategies with Options, forex , day trading and Swing Trading.

Make a outstanding profit following basic strategies in the short term and avoiding the overnight collapse

© Copyright 2021 by Cal Long

Table of contents

TRADING OPTION 1
Table of contents 2
Chapter 1 6
   What's an Option Contract? 6
      1.1 Now, how does an option Contracts Work? 6
      1.2 Make use of stock options for the listed objectives: 8
      1.3 Why does an option contract matter? 10
Chapter2 11
   The various options trading jargon. 11
      2.1 Stock option quotes 12
      2.3 Explanation of what an option may be worth 14
      2.4 Options buyer and seller term conditions 15
Chapter 3 17
   What's a Strike Price? 17
      3.1 KEYNOTE 17
      3.2 Understanding Strike Prices 17
      3.3 Strike Price Example 19
Chapter 4 21
   TOP REASONS TO TRADE OPTIONS 21
      4.1 Buy Option Explanation 21
      4.2 Buy Option Example 22
      4.3 Application of Purchase Options 23
      4.4 The benefits of Options 25

Chapter 5 33
Covered calls 33
5.1 Understanding Covered Calls 34
5.2 Covered Call Example 36
5.3 One of the two scenarios will play out: 36
Chapter 6 39
Call Buying Strategy 39
6.1 Call Buying 40
Chapter 7 42
Volatility in the markets 42
7.1 Investment in Volatile Market 43
7.2 How Trading is affected during periods of Volatility. 44
Chapter 8 45
In the money out of the money 45
8.1 In the Money 46
8.2 Out of the money 48
8.3 Exactly how Put Options Work 49
8.4 Just how Put Options Priced Are? 50
8.5 Buying vs. Selling Put Options 51
Chapter 9 53
Beginners common mistakes 53
Chapter 10 58
Advanced trading strategies 58
10.1 Conclusion 71

© Copyright 2021 by Cal Long

All rights reserved. No part of this guide may be reproduced in any form without permission in writing from the publisher except in the case of brief quotations embodied in critical articles or reviews.

Legal & Disclaimer

The information contained in this book and its contents is not designed to replace or take the place of any form of medical or professional advice; and is not meant to replace the need for independent medical, financial, legal or other professional advice or services, as may be required. The content and information in this book have been provided for educational and entertainment purposes only.

The content and information contained in this book has been compiled from sources deemed reliable, and it is accurate to the best of the Author's knowledge, information and belief. However, the Author cannot guarantee its accuracy and validity and cannot be held liable for any errors and/or omissions. Further, changes are periodically made to this book as and when needed. Where appropriate and/or necessary, you must consult a professional (including but not limited to your doctor, attorney, financial advisor or such other professional advisor) before using any of the suggested remedies, techniques, or information in this book.

Upon using the contents and information contained in this book, you agree to hold harmless the Author from and against any damages, costs, and expenses, including any legal fees potentially resulting from the application of any of the information provided by this book. This disclaimer applies to any loss, damages or injury caused by the use and application, whether directly or indirectly, of any advice or information presented, whether for breach of contract, tort, negligence, personal injury, criminal intent, or under any other cause of action.

You agree to accept all risks of using the information presented inside this book.

You agree that by continuing to read this book, where appropriate and/or necessary, you shall consult a professional (including but not limited to your doctor, attorney, or financial advisor or such other advisor as needed) before using any of the suggested remedies, techniques, or information in this book.

Chapter 1

What's an Option Contract?

An option agreement is an understanding between a purchaser as well as a seller, which provides the purchaser with the possibility, best to purchase or even promote a specific advantage later on in an agreed-upon price. Options contracts are usually used in securities, real estate transactions, and commodities.

1.1 Now, how does an option Contracts Work?

There are many kinds of choices contracts in monetary transactions. An exchange-traded choice, for instance, is a standardized agreement that is settled by way of a clearinghouse, and it is assured. These exchange-traded choices cover stock options, futures options, and index options, interest rate options, bonds, and commodity options. Yet another kind of selection agreement is an over-the-counter option that is a trade-in between two different private parties. This might consist of interest rate choices, currency exchange fee options, along with swaps (i.e., trading long as well as short terms interest rates).

The primary options that come with an exchange-traded choice, like a call choices contract, give a right to purchase a hundred shares of a security at a certain price by a set date. The choices shrink charges a market-based charge (called a premium). The stock price mentioned in the agreement is known as the "strike cost." In the same period, a put choices contract provides the customer of the contract the right to promote the inventory in a hit cost by a chosen date. In both instances, if the customer of the choices contract doesn't act by the designated day, the possibility it expires.

A financial option is described as a contractual agreement that exists between two parties. Even though some option contracts are over the counter, which means they're somewhere between two people without starting an exchange, standardized contracts recognized as listed options trade on the exchange. Option contracts provide owner rights as well as seller obligations. Allow me to share the primary key definitions as well as details:

Call option: A call choice provides the owner (seller) the best (obligation) to purchase (sell) a certain amount of shares of the basic stock at a certain cost by a predetermined date. A call choice offers you the chance to make money from cost gains in the basic stock in a portion of the expense of owning the inventory.

Put option: Put choices provide the owner (seller) the best (obligation) to offer (buy) a certain amount of shares of the basic stock at a certain cost by a certain date. When you have put option on a stock that you to promote, so the cost of the stock is dropping, the put choice is getting in worth, thus offsetting the losses on the inventory and also providing you with a chance to make choices regarding the stock ownership of yours without panicking.

Rights of the owner of a choices contract: A call choice provides the owner the best to purchase a certain amount of shares of stock in a predetermined value. A put choice provides the owner of it's the best to market a certain amount of shares of stock in a predetermined value.

Responsibilities of a choices seller: Sellers of call choices hold the obligation to market a certain amount of shares of the basic stock in a predetermined value. Sellers of put options hold the obligation to purchase a certain amount of stock at a predetermined price.

1.2 Make use of stock options for the listed objectives:

• To gain from upside moves for a lesser amount of money

• To benefit from downside movements in stocks without the threat of small selling

• To protect a private stock position or maybe a full portfolio during times of falling prices as well as market downturns

1.4 How to be conscious of the risk of trading options.

Listed here are two key concepts:

1. Options contracts have a restricted life: Each contract comes with an expiration date. That suggests if the move you foresee is near to the expiration date, you are going to lose the entire initial investment. You can discover exactly how these things happen by paper trading before you are doing it in real-time.

Paper trading allows you to test several choices for the underlying stock, doing two things. One is the fact that you can see what goes on in the time that is real—seeing what -happens, in turn, allows you to determine how you can choose the most effective choice and the way to handle the placement.

2. The wrong Strategy can result in disastrous results: When you bring much more risk than needed, you are going to limit the rewards of yours and expose yourself to limitless losses. This's the identical thing that is going to occur when you sold stocks short, which could wipe out the goal of trading option. Specific option strategies and options allow you to accomplish the same as selling stocks short (profiting from a lessening of prices of the underlying asset) in a portion of the price.

For instance, in an easy call option contrast, a trader might anticipate Company XYZ's stock price going up as many as 90 dollars in the following month. The trader views that he can purchase a choice contract of company XYZ at dollar 4.50 with a strike price of 95 dollars per share. The trader should pay the price of an opportunity ($ 4.50 X hundred shares = $ 450). The stock price starts to grow as expected as well as stabilizes at 100 dollars. Before the expiry day on the choices contract, the trader executes the call choice and buys a hundred shares of Company XYZ during 95 dollars, the strike price on the options contract o. He pays $ 7,500 for the stock. The trader may subsequently promote the new stock of his today for $ 10,000, producing a $ 2,050 benefit ($ 2,500 minus $ 450 for the options contract).

1.3 Why does an option contract matter?

Option contracts are a crucial tool giving traders the chance to hedge the stock positions of theirs. Choices permit a leveraged placement on stock while mitigating the chance of the total purchase. Likewise, for the property, an option contract might permit a purchaser to secure choice contracts on several parcels before needing to perform the investment on any single one, making sure the customer will have the ability to create all of them before going ahead.

Chapter2

The various options trading jargon.

The Contracts, Calls, Puts, premium, Strike price, Intrinsic worth, time worth, In and out of money in options trading.

These are the languages of options traders - a riddled jargon dialect of conventional Wall Street-speak.

Becoming conversant very first requires learning a couple of key terms. This book will share the necessities of options trading terms for starting investors.

1. Option type: You will find two types of options you can buy or sell:

<u>Call</u>: an option contract that provides you with the right to purchase stock at a set price within a particular period.

<u>Put</u> an option contract that provides you with the right to promote stock at a set price within a particular period.

2. Expiration date: The day once the options shrink will become void. It is the due date for you to perform a thing together with the agreement, and yes, it may be many days, weeks, years, or months down the road.

3. The strike price, or maybe exercise price: The cost at which you can purchase or sell the stock in case you opt to exercise the possibility.

4. Premium: The per-share price you spend on an option. The high quality consists of:

Intrinsic worth: The worth of an option depending on the big difference between a stock's present market price and also the option's strike selling price.

Time worth: The worth of an alternative according to the quantity of time before the contract expires. Time is valuable to investors due to the chance that an option's intrinsic value increases throughout the contract's precious time frame. As the expiration date becomes nearer, time value decreases. This is known as time decay or maybe "theta," following the choices pricing model used to compute it.

2.1 Stock option quotes

Call up an inventory quote, and also you find the present market share cost of the organization the quantity you would spend when you purchased shares or maybe the total amount you would get if you sold them. Quotes for option contracts are a great deal much more complicated since several designs are offered to exchange grounded on the type, expiration date, strike cost, and much more.

Strike: The cost you would pay or receive if you exercised the possibility.

Contract name: Just love stocks have ticker symbols, alternatives contracts have choice symbols with letters as well as numbers which match to the specifics in a contract. In a genuine option chain, the company's ticker sign will occur before the agreement name.

Finally: The cost which was paid or received the final time the possibility was traded.

Bid: The cost a purchaser is prepared to purchase the possibility. If you are selling an option, this is the premium you would receive because of the contract.

Ask The cost a seller is prepared to accept for the feature. If you would like to get an option, this is the premium you would pay.

Change: The cost change after the prior trading day is closed, likewise conveyed in portion terms.

Volume: The actual number of contracts traded for the given day.

Open interest: The amount of options contracts already in play.

Volatility: A measurement of just how much a stock priced moves in between the low and high cost daily. Historical Volatility, as the title suggests, is calculated using previous cost information. It may be assessed on an annual basis or perhaps while in a particular time frame.

Implied "IV," or Volatility in options quote shorthand, measures just how likely it's the marketplace thinks a stock will encounter a price tag swing. (You additionally may audibly hear of "vega," the choice pricing model used to determine the theoretical impact which each one-point change in the stock price tag has on Implied Volatility.)

Higher implied Volatility generally means higher choice costs due to a higher likely upside for the agreement. But do not take these computations as certainties. Just like earnings estimates are simply an analyst's prediction of exactly what a business is apt to make, volatility procedures are just predictions about precisely how a great deal of an option's cost might change.

2.3 Explanation of what an option may be worth

With regards to describing options overall performance, saying "up," "down," or maybe "flat" does not cut it. Within any time that an options agreement is in play, it's among three things:

In the money: This describes a choice which has intrinsic value - if the connection between stock cost in the open market as well as the strike price favors the choices shrink owner If the stock price tag is bigger compared to the strike price that is news that is good for the proprietor of a call option. A put choice is in the cash in case the stock price tag is lower compared to the strike price.

Out of the money: When there is no financial advantage to exercising the alternative, it is called from the cash. Practically speaking, an out-of-the-money alternative produces purchasing or even selling shares in the strike cost much less profitable than paying for or perhaps selling on the open market. A call choice is out of the cash in case the stock price tag is lower compared to the strike price. A put choice is out of the cash whenever the stock price is higher compared to the strike price.

At the money: If the stock price is roughly comparable to the strike price, an alternative is considered in cash. Essentially, it is a wash.

2.4 Options buyer and seller term conditions

These final two cover varieties of options traders. This is another case where conventional terms as "buyer" and "seller" do not capture the nuances of options trading.

Holder: Describes the investor that has a choice contract. A call holder pays for the option to purchase the inventory, depending on the variables of the agreement. A put holder has got the right to promote the stock.

Writer: Describes the investor who's promoting the choices contract. The author gets the high quality from the holder in return for the promise to purchase and promote the specified shares in the strike price if the holder exercises the option. Besides being on opposing sides of the transaction, the largest distinction between option slots as well as option authors is the exposure to risk.

Remember, holders, are buying the proper to buy and sell shares, though they are not obligated to do anything at all. Their agreement grants them the independence to determine when - or even if - to work out the option, or to market the agreement just before it expires. When they wind up with an out-of-the-money option, they could walk away and allow the contract to expire. They drop just how much they spent on the choice (the premium) as well as the expense of industry profits.

Freelance writers do not have that flexibility. For instance, when a call holder chooses to work out an option, the author is required to satisfy the order and promote the inventory in the strike price. In case the author does not currently have adequate shares of the inventory, he will need to purchase shares in the heading market price - even when it is much higher compared to the strike priced - and also promote them at a loss on the call holder.

Due to the limitless downside possibilities, we suggest that investors just starting in choices stick on the purchasing (holding) side before venturing into much more advanced option trading methods.

Chapter 3

What's a Strike Price?

A strike price will be the set price at which a derivative agreement is purchased or even offered when it's worked out. For the call option, the strike prices are exactly where the security could be purchased by an opportunity holder; for a put option, the strike price will be the cost at that the security could be offered. Strike prices are likewise known as the physical exercise price.

3.1 KEYNOTE

• Strike cost is the cost at which a derivative agreement can be purchased or even offered (exercised).

• Derivatives are monetary items whose worth is based (derived) on the underlying asset, typically an additional economic instrument.

• The strike price, likewise referred to as physical exercise price, would be the most crucial determinant of the selected printer.

3.2 Understanding Strike Prices

Strike costs are utilized in derivatives (mainly options) Trading. Derivatives are monetary items whose worth is based (derived) on the underlying asset, typically an additional economic instrument. The strike price is a critical variable of call and puts options. For instance, the customer of a stock option call will have the proper, although not the obligation, to purchase that inventory in the future at the strike price. Similarly, the customer of a stock choice put would have the proper, although not the obligation, to promote that stock down in the future at the strike price.

The strike or maybe training price is the most crucial determinant of option printer. Strike costs are determined if a contract is first written. It informs the investor what cost the underlying asset should achieve before the choice is in-the-money (ITM). Strike costs are standardized, which means they're at fixed dollar amounts, for example, $31, $105, $102.50, $33, $32, etc.

The cost difference between the underlying stock price as well as the strike price establishes an option's price. For customers of a call option, if the strike price tag is above the basic stock price, the option is from the cash (OTM). In this particular situation, the possibility does not have intrinsic worth. However, it might still have a great dependence on time and Volatility until expiration, as either of these two elements might place the option in cash down the road. Alternatively, if the basic stock prices are above the strike price, the choice is going to have intrinsic value and also have the investment.

A purchaser of a put option is going to be in the cash whenever the underlying stock prices are beneath the strike cost and also be from the cash when the underlying stock prices are above the strike price. Once again, an OTM alternative will not have intrinsic worth. However, it might still have great depending on the Volatility of the underlying asset as well as the time remaining until selection expiration.

3.3 Strike Price Example

Assume you will find two option contracts. It is a call option with a hundred dollars strike selling price. An alternative is a call option with a $ 150 strike selling price. The present cost of the underlying stock is $ 145. Assume both call choices will be the same; the sole difference will be the strike price.

At expiration, the very first agreement may be worth 45 dollars. That's, it's in cash by 45 dollars. This is since the stock is trading $45 higher compared to the strike price.

The other agreement is out of the cash by $5. When the selling price of the underlying asset is beneath the call's hit price at expiration, the possibility expires worthless.

If perhaps we've two put options, both about to expire, plus you have a strike price of $ 40 and also the various other features a strike price of $50, we can appear on the present stock price to discover that option has worth. Whenever the basic stock is trading at $45, the $50 put option has a $5 price since the underlying stock is beneath the strike cost of the put.

The forty dollars put choice does not have any worth, because the basic stock is above the strike price. Recall that put choices allow the option buyer to market at the strike price. There's simply no stage using the choice to market at $40 when they can sell at $45 in the stock market. Thus, the $40 strike price placed is worthless at expiration.

Chapter 4

TOP REASONS TO TRADE OPTIONS

Buy option, described as the chance to buy a portion of the property that is being leased following the lease is ended, is an element of the countless options offered in a lease agreement. A purchase option is usually agreed upon by the two parties involved before the contract is made.

4.1 Buy Option Explanation

Buy option, defined by a lot of businesspeople as an option to "try it before you purchase it," can be purchased on nearly every leased advantage. The importance of a lease buys an alternative contract is apparent. A party wants to lease a portion of equipment since it cannot afford to purchase it. Nevertheless, to help keep the options open, they need to buy an option lease. This benefits the lessor by enabling her to choose, at the last time, if the product has produced worth, and it is worth keeping. Furthermore, the lessor can account for changes in operations, expectations, or needs by leaving the options of their open and choosing a purchase option.

For the lessee, it enables them to think of the earnings from leasing the product while simultaneously making the income from offering the product. This way, a buy option offers again to both parties. Additionally, it allows access to and earnings from the asset almost instantly. A purchase option fee might be accrued while choosing to participate in these kinds of contracts.

4.2 Buy Option Example

Asal is renting a portion of pieces of equipment for the graphic printing firm. Asal, due to the vast equipment needed, she has to make sure that the money flows important to operate the business according to the present needs. She presently cannot afford to get this piece of gear. Nevertheless, she sees the worth in having it accessible in the office. Asal balances these two needs by agreeing on a buy option with the entire lessor.

Asal is developing a short term agreement to lease the piece of gear, a business quality printer available. She is going to keep this printer in the office for one year, after which she'll purchase the product, as well as her lessor, agree on the good market value for the printer. Therefore, Asal completes the investment option agreement and starts to use the product.

One year later, Asal was now seeing a great deal of growth in the business of her. A great deal of growth, she's likely to outsource the printing for the customers of her to a much better-equipped company. She trusts this particular vendor and understands the quality of the goods they create; therefore, she trusts the business.

This particular change of tempo negates the need of her to buy the printer she was leasing. Asal is nearing the conclusion of the lease agreement of her; therefore, she informs the lessor which she won't be accepting the investment option after the lease. She's crucial expenditures making at this time.

Asal is satisfied she produced a purchase agreement. She made the best business decision and will quickly see the fruits of the labor. She opens work the following day with the sensation of achievement.

4.3 Application of Purchase Options

The investment option is a flexible application that may be put on to a selection of purposes: • Buying period. Land trusts three typically require years or months to raise money for any conservation project. A buy option provides the land trust time to get funding with no fear that the property is going to be sold or even created in the meantime. Additionally, it guarantees the land trust in which the raised money will visit the intended purpose of theirs since the investment option legally obligates the owners to close the transaction in the stipulated time and price.

• Reducing danger. A land trust might tentatively determine a home as very crucial that you shed but can't threat buy before a comprehensive investigation establishes it's a good preservation investment; for instance, the purchase price is regulatory and appropriate issues are manageable or absent.

• Assembling parcels. A task could count on the acquisition of several parcels of easements or land to complete the desired preservation objectives. A land trust might be using buy option to get control with the attributes parcel by parcel without being required to buy the home interests, doing this just when it's able, willing, and ready to buy all of the crucial interests.

• Handling disorganized ownership scenarios. In case the owners are certainly not of one mind about the future of their generally owned property or perhaps are not talking with each other, the investment option might be utilized to obtain individuals from each the best to purchase the percentage interest of theirs in the land. The land trust isn't obliged to buy any of the portion interests, doing this only when it's able, willing, and ready to buy the property in the entirety of its.

• Incentivizing action. The time-limited character of a buy option might be utilized to produce a feeling of opportunity as well as the urgency that inspires a community as well as donors to act before the opportunity passes.

• Compensating for lost ability. An owner might need dollars to compensate for keeping the property of his away from the market for the gain of the land trust. To this conclusion, the investment alternative might be organized to offer cash payments, either initial or perhaps in installments, to the owner.

- Controlling results. The option can be utilized to ensure that promises are maintained and expectations recognized. For instance, a land trust that transfers home to a local government might prefer a function to reacquire the home for a below-market or nominal worth in case the government's promises to make use of the ground just for preservation and outdoor public recreation aren't maintained.

4.4 The benefits of Options

They've existed for over 40 years, though options are just today starting to get the interest they deserve. A lot of investors have keep away from choices, believing them being advanced and also, consequently, very hard to realize. A lot of more have had bad first happenings with option because neither they neither their brokers were adequately taught in exactly how to utilize them. The improper use of the option, that way of any effective tool, could lead to significant problems.

Lastly, words as "risky" or maybe "dangerous" were improperly connected to option by the financial media plus certain famous figures on the market. Nevertheless, the unique investor needs to get each side of the story before making an option about the worth of options.

You will find four important advantages (in no specific order) option might give an investor:

They might offer increased cost-efficiency

They could be less risky compared to equities

They can provide higher percentage returns

They provide a selection of strategic options with benefits such as these; you can find out how people who are utilizing choices for some time will be at a loss to explain options' not enough recognition.

Let us check into these benefits one by one.

1. Cost-Efficiency

An option has excellent leveraging power. As a result, an investor can get an option job much like a stock job, but at big cost savings. For instance, to buy 200 shares of an $80 inventory, an investor should shell out $16,000. Nevertheless, if the investor were purchasing $22 calls (with every agreement that represents a hundred shares), the complete cost will be just $4,000 (2 contracts x 100 shares/contract x $20 market price). The investor would later have one more $ 12,000 to work with at his or maybe the discretion of her.

It's more or less not as easy as that. The investor must choose the proper call to buy (a subject for another discussion) to imitate the inventory job accurately. Nevertheless, this Strategy referred to as stock replacement, isn't just viable but cost-efficient and practical also.

Example

Say you want to buy Schlumberger (SLB) since you feel it'll be going up through the following several months. You need to purchase 200 shares while SLB is trading at $131; this will set you back a total of $ 26,200. Rather than adding up that much cash, you can go into the choices sector, picked an opportunity mimicking the stock carefully, and purchased the August call choice, with a strike price of $100, for $44. To get a position equivalent in dimension on the

200 shares stated previously, you will have to purchase two contracts. This will provide your total purchase to $6,800 (two contracts x hundred shares/contract x $34market price), instead of $ 26,200. The real difference might be left in the account of yours to gain interest or even be put on to the next opportunity providing much better diversification possibilities, among various other things.

2. Less Risk

Right now, there are circumstances in which buying choices are riskier than having equities, but additionally, there are instances when alternatives could be utilized to reduce risk. It truly depends on the way you utilize them. An option could be much less risky for investors since they need much less monetary dedication compared to equities, plus they may additionally be less risky because of their relative imperviousness on the likely catastrophic consequences of gap openings.

An option would be the most reliable type of hedge, which also makes them safer compared to stocks. When an investor buys stocks, a stop-loss order is often positioned to protect the placement. The stop order is created to stop losses beneath a predetermined cost displaying the investor. The issue with such orders is based on the dynamics of the order itself. A stop order is performed once the stock trades at or perhaps below the cap, as suggested in the order.

For instance, we need to say you purchase a stock at $55. You don't want to lose any greater than 10 % of the investment of yours; therefore, you set a $45stop order. This particular order is going to become a market order to market after the stock trades at or even under $45. This order works throughout the day, though it might result in problems at night. Let's say you head to bed with the stock having shut at $51. The following morning, if you awaken and switch on CNBC, you pick up that there's news that is breaking on the stock of yours. It appears the company's CEO is lying about the earnings reports for quite a while today, and you can also find rumors of embezzlement. The stock is anticipated to open down around $20. When that happens, $20 will be the very first swap beneath your stop order's $45 limit selling price. Thus, once the stock opens, you market at $20, locking in a significant loss. The stop-loss order wasn't there for you if you needed it most.

Had you bought a put option for safety, you'd not have endured the catastrophic loss. Unlike stop-loss orders, options don't turn off once the market closes. They provide you with insurance twenty-four hours one day, seven days a week. This is a thing stop order cannot do. This is precisely why options are believed to be a reliable form of hedging.

Moreover, as a substitute for buying the inventory, you can have used the method pointed out previously (stock replacement), in which you buy an in-the-money call rather than buying the inventory. Several options mimic as many as 80% of a stock's performance, but price one quarter the cost of the inventory. If you'd purchased the $45 strike call rather than the stock, the loss of yours would be confined to everything you spent on the choice. In case you paid $6 for the option, you will have lost just $6, not the $31 you would shed if you had the stock. The usefulness of stop orders pales in comparison to the organic, full-time stop provided by choices.

3. Higher Potential Returns

You do not require a calculator to discover in case you spend less and make practically the same revenue, and you will have a better percentage return. If they pay off, that is what options usually offer to investors.

For instance, making use of the scenario from above, we will compare the portion earnings of the stock (purchased for $50) as well as the choice (purchased at $60). Let us state the possibility carries a delta of eighty, which means the option's value is going to change 80 % of the stock's price shift. When the stock was going up to $5, the stock position of yours will provide a 10 % return. The options position of yours would acquire 80% of the stock movement (due to its eighty delta), or perhaps $5. A $4 gain on a $6 buy amounts to a 67 % return - a lot better than the 10 % return on the inventory.

Naturally, if the trade does not go the way of yours, options can exact a huge toll: there's the possibility you are going to lose 100% of the investment of yours.

4. More Strategic Alternatives

The last main advantage of options is they provide more investment alternatives. Choices are a rather adaptable tool. You can find numerous ways to make use of options to recreate various other positions. We call these jobs synthetics.

Synthetic positions contained investors with numerous ways to achieve the very same choice objectives, which can be invaluable. While synthetic positions are believed to be an enhanced option topic, alternatives offer many other strategic alternatives. For instance, a lot of investors wear brokers that ask a margin when an investor would like to short a stock. The price of this margin requirement is extremely prohibitive. Some other investors implement brokers who just don't enable the shorting of stocks, period. The failure to enjoy the drawback, if needed, essentially handcuffs investors and causes them right into a black-and-white society as the industry trades in color. But no broker has some rule against investors purchasing places to enjoy the drawback, and this is an obvious advantage of option trading.

The utilization of options likewise allows for the investor to trade the market's "third dimension," when you'll - no course. Options enable the investor to trade not just stock movements but additionally the passage of movements and time in Volatility. The majority of stocks do not have large moves for the majority of the time. Just a couple of stocks move significantly, and they get it done seldom. The ability of yours to make use of stagnation may grow to be the aspect of deciding whether the financial goals of yours are reached, or maybe they stay just a pipe dream. Only options provide the strategic option required to profit in each market type.

Chapter 5

Covered calls

What's a Covered Call?

A covered call describes a transaction in the economic market place where the investor promoting call option has the equivalent level of the underlying security. To perform the investor holding an extended position in an asset subsequently writes (sells) call selections on that very same advantage to create an income stream. The investor's lengthy position of the advantage is the "cover" since it indicates the seller can provide the shares in case the customer of the call option chooses to work out.

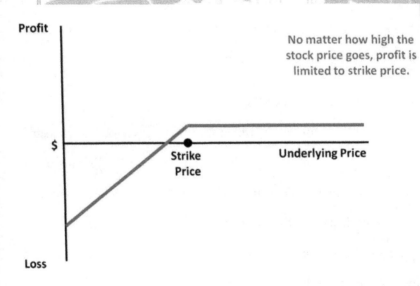

Whenever the investor instantly buys inventory and also writes call options against that inventory job, it's widely known as a "buy-write" transaction.

Key elements

A covered call is a favorite option approach used to produce income in the type of choice premiums.

To perform a covered call, an investor holding an extended position in an asset subsequently writes (sells) call selections on that same advantage.

It's frequently employed by people who intend to support the underlying stock for a very long time but don't expect a definite price rise in the near term.

This particular method is perfect for an investor that believes the underlying price won't move much over the near term.

5.1 Understanding Covered Calls

Covered calls are a basic approach, which means the investor just expects a small decrease or increase in the underlying stock cost for the lifetime of the created call option. This particular method is usually used when an investor has a short-term basic perspective on the asset, and because of this, keeps the asset simultaneously and long carries a brief position through the option to produce income out of the choice premium.

To put it simply, in case an investor intends to support the underlying stock for a very long time but doesn't anticipate an appreciable cost rise in the near term well, and then they can produce income (premiums) for the account of theirs even though they wait out the lull.

A covered call can serve as a short-term hedge over much stock job and also allows investors to generate income through the premium received for composing the possibility. Nevertheless, the investor forfeits inventory profits in case the cost moves above the option strike selling price. They're additionally required to offer a hundred shares in the strike price (for each agreement written) in case the customer chooses to work out the possibility.

A covered call tactic isn't helpful for neither an extremely bullish nor an extremely bearish investor. If an investor is quite bullish, they're usually better off not writing the option and simply holding the stock. The option caps the benefit on the inventory, which could decrease the general revenue of the industry in case the stock price spikes. Likewise, in case an investor is quite bearish, they could be more well off merely selling the inventory since the premium gotten for composing a call option is going to do very little to counterbalance the damage on the stock when the stock plummets.

Maximum Loss and Profit The optimum benefit associated with a covered call is the same as the strike cost of the short call option, much less the purchase cost of the underlying stock, and also the premium received.

The optimum loss is the same as the price of the basic stock, much less the premium received.

5.2 Covered Call Example

An investor owns shares of hypothetical business TSJ. They love its long-lasting prospects in addition to the share price of its but think in the shorter term the stock will probably trade fairly flat, maybe within a few dollars of the current price of its $25.

When they offer a call choice on TSJ with a strike price of $27, they generate the high quality out of the option sale but, because of the length of the possibility, cap the upside of theirs on the stock to $27. Assume the premium they get for writing a three-month phone call choice is 1dolar1 0.75 ($75.per contract or maybe a hundred shares).

5.3 One of the two scenarios will play out:

TSJ shares trade beneath the t$27 strike selling price. The option is going to expire uselessly, and also the investor will maintain the premium from the feature. In this particular situation, by utilizing the buy-write approach, they've effectively outperformed the inventory. They still wear the stock but have an additional $75in the pocket of theirs, fewer fees.

TSJ shares rise above twenty-seven dollars. The possibility is worked out, and also the benefit in the stock is capped at $27. When price moves above $ 27.75

(strike cost along with premium), the investor could have been more well off positioning the inventory. Although, in case they planned to market at $27 anyway, publishing the call choice gave them an additional $0.75 a share.

Buying calls (you require image) The popular myth that 90 % of all choices expire worthlessly frightens investors into wrongly thinking that in case they purchase choices, they will lose money 90 % of the period. But in truth, the Chicago Board Options Exchange (CBOE) estimates that just approximately 30 % of choices expire worthless, while 10 % are worked out, and the other 60 % are traded away or perhaps shut by building an offsetting spot.

Key elements

• Buying calls, then selling, or even exercising them for an income is usually a great method to boost your portfolio's efficiency.

• Investors frequently purchase calls when they're bullish for other security or stock since it affords them leverage.

- Call choices help lessen the optimum damage an asset might incur, unlike stocks, exactly where the whole value of the purchase might be forfeited if the stock price drops to zero.

Chapter 6

Call Buying Strategy

Whenever you purchase a call, you spend the choice premium in return for the appropriate to purchase shares at a fixed cost (strike cost) on or perhaps before a particular day (expiration date). Investors most often purchase calls when they're bullish on other security or stock since it provides leverage.

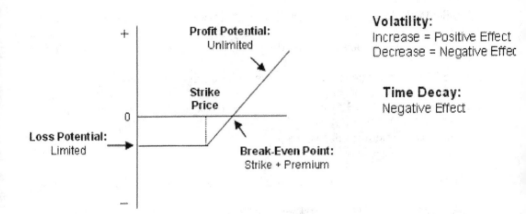

For instance, assume XYZ stock trades for $50. A one-month call option on the stock fees $3. Would you quite purchase a hundred shares of XYZ for $5,000, or perhaps might you rather purchase one call option for $ 300 ($3x hundred shares), with the payoff being determined by the stock 's closing price one month from today? Imagine the graphic illustration of the two various scenarios below.

6.1 Call Buying

As you can see, the payoff for every investment differs. While purchasing the stock is going to require an asset of $5,000, you can manage an identical amount of shares for only $300 by purchasing a call option. Likewise, remember the breakeven cost on the stock industry is $50 per share, while the breakeven price on the choice trade is $53 per share (not factoring in fees or commissions).

While both investments have limitless upside possibilities in the month following the purchase of theirs, the possible loss scenarios are vastly different. Case in point: While the greatest possible damage on the choice is $300, the damage on the stock buy could be the whole $5,000 first purchase, should the share price tag plummet to zero.

To close the Position, Investors might close out the call positions of theirs by offering them to the marketplace or perhaps with them worked out, in which case they have to send dollars on the counterparties that sold them.

Continuing with the example of ours, let's assume the stock was trading at $55 near the one-month expiration. Under this particular set of situations, you can sell the call of yours for roughly $500 ($5x hundred shares), which could provide you with net revenue of $200 ($500 minus the $300 premium).

Conversely, you can hold the call exercised; in that case, you will be obligated to spend $5,000 ($5x hundred shares) as well as the counterparty that sold you the call would provide the shares. With this particular strategy, the return would likewise be $ 200 ($5,500 $ 5,000 $ 300 $ 200). Remember that the payoff from training and promoting the call is the same net benefit of $200.

Chapter 7

Volatility in the markets

What's Volatility?

Volatility is a statistical measure of the inclination of a market or maybe protection to climb and fall sharply within a quick time. It's usually assessed by the conventional deviation of the substitution of an investment. The regular deviation is a statistical idea that denotes the quantity of variation or maybe deviation, which may be expected.

Volatile markets tend to be characterized by wide cost fluctuations as well as major Trading. They frequently end up from an imbalance of industry orders in a single direction (for instance, most buys and absolutely no sales). Others point out volatile market places are induced by such things as financial releases, business news, a suggestion from a popular analyst, a famous initial public offering (Unexpected earnings) benefits. Others blame Volatility on day traders, institutional investors, and short-sellers.

One explanation is the fact that investor reactions are triggered by psychological forces. This particular principle flies in the face of an effective industry hypothesis (EMH) that says that market charges are right and change to focus all info. This particular behavioral method states that sizable cost changes (Volatility) result from a collective change of mind by the investing public. There's absolutely no consensus about what brings about Volatility, nonetheless, since Volatility and investors should develop methods to cope with it.

7.1 Investment in Volatile Market

One of the ways to cope with Volatility is avoiding it entirely. This means staying invested but not paying attention to short term fluctuations. Occasionally this is often tougher than it sounds; you watch your portfolio take a 50% knock in a bear market could be much more than most should take.

One common misconception in regards to a buy-and-hold strategy is the fact that holding a stock for 20 years is what'll make you cash. Long-term investing nevertheless demands homework because marketplaces are driven by corporate basics. In case you discover a company with a solid balance sheet as well as uniform earnings, the short-term fluctuations will not affect the long-term value of the business. In reality, periods of Volatility may be a good time to buy should you think a business is great for the long term.

The primary argument behind the buy-and-hold program is the fact that missing the very best couple of days of the entire year will cut the return of yours significantly. It differs based on the place you get the data of yours, but the statistic will often sound something such as this: "missing the twenty greatest days can cut the return of yours by much more than half." For probably the most part, this is real. But then again, lacking the most detrimental twenty times will even improve the portfolio of yours significantly. In several instances, you might wish to make trades during volatile market conditions.

7.2 How Trading is affected during periods of Volatility.

Investors, particularly those involving an internet broker, must understand that during periods of Volatility, numerous firms implement methods that are created to reduce the publicity of the firm to remarkable industry danger. For instance, in the past, several market maker firms have temporarily discontinued standard instant order executions and also managed orders by hand.

How securities are executed during periods of high volume and volatile prices are additionally different in different ways.

The following factors below are needed to be taken into consideration:

Waiting times: Volatile marketplaces are connected with high volumes of Trading, which might result in delays in execution. These high volumes might also result in executions to take place for prices, which are drastically distinct from the market price quoted in the time the purchase was entered. Investors must ask firms to explain exactly how to market creators handle order executions if the market is volatile. With all the proliferation of internet trading, we've come to expect fast executions at costs at or close to the quotes displayed on the internet-enabled devices of ours. Take into consideration this is not often the truth.

<u>Electronic Mayhem:</u> You might have difficulties performing the trades of yours due to the limits of a system 's capacity. Additionally, in case you're trading online, you might have difficulty accessing the account of yours because of the high levels of online visitors. For these reasons, the majority of internet trading firms provide alternate options as phone trades or even speaking with a broker on the phone to begin an order.

<u>Incorrect Quotes:</u> There may be considerable cost discrepancies between the quote you get as well as the price at which the trade of yours is executed. Don't forget, in a volatile industry atmosphere; possibly real-time quotes might be far behind what's presently taking place on the market. Additionally, the number of shares offered at a particular price (known as the dimensions of a quote) might change quickly, impacting the chance of a quoted cost being offered for you.

Chapter 8

In the money out of the money

In options trading, the big difference between "in the money" (ITM) and also "out of the money" (OTM) is a situation of the strike price's position relative to the market valuation of the underlying stock, named the moneyless of its.

An ITM option is but one with a strike price that has currently been surpassed by the present stock price. An OTM choice is a single which has a strike cost that the underlying security has yet to achieve, which means the possibility does not have intrinsic value.

8.1 In the Money

ITM option has thier uses. For instance, a trader may wish to hedge or even partially hedge the position of theirs. They might additionally need to buy an option which has several intrinsic values, and not only time value. As ITM choices have intrinsic worth and are valued more compared to OTM option in the same chain, the cost moves (%) are fairly smaller. That's not saying ITM option will not have big price movements, they can and do, but, as compared to OTM choices, the portion techniques are smaller.

Specific techniques call for ITM choices, while others call for OTM choices, and quite often both. One isn't superior to another; it simply comes right down to the things that work for the very best for the technique in question.

A call option provides the choice customer the best to buy shares at the strike price in case it's helpful to do it. An in the cash call option, consequently, is one that has a strike price lower compared to the present stock price. A call option which has a strike price of $ 132.50, for instance, is seen as ITM when the basic stock is estimated at $ 135 per share as the strike price tag has been surpassed. A call option which has a strike price higher than $135 will be regarded as OTM because the stock hasn't yet come to the level.

In the situation of the stock trading at $135, and also the choice hit of $132.50, the choice would've $2.50 worth of intrinsic worth, though the choice might cost $5to purchase. It costs five dollars because there's $ 2.50 of the rest, and the intrinsic value of the possible cost, considered the premium, is made up of time value. You pay much more for time worth the further the choice is from expiry as the basic stock price is going to move before expiry, which offers a chance to the chosen customer as well as the threat to the choice writer that they have been compensated for.

Put choices are bought by traders that feel the stock price goes down. ITM put options, consequently, are the ones that have strike prices above the present stock price. A put alternative with a strike price of seventy-five dollars is in the cash when the basic stock is estimated at seventy-two dollars because the stock price tag has relocated beneath the strike. That very same put alternative will be out of the cash when the basic stock is trading at eighty dollars.

In cash, option offers a greater premium than not cash choices, due to the time value problem described above.

8.2 Out of the money

In the money or from the money option, both have their cons and pros. One isn't superior to the other person. Instead, the different strike prices in a choice chain accommodate all kinds of traders as well as options strategies.

With regards to purchasing options, which are OTM or ITM, the option is dependent upon the outlook of yours for the underlying security, economic situation, and even what you're attempting to attain.

OTM choices are more affordable compared to ITM choices, which in turn permits them to be more inviting to traders with very little capital. Although trading on a shoestring budget isn't suggested. Several of the uses for OTM choices include purchasing the choices in case you want a huge action in the stock. Since OTM choices have a reduced up the front price (no intrinsic value) than ITM choices, purchasing an OTM choice is a fair option. In case a stock presently trades at a hundred dollars, you can purchase an OTM call alternative with a hit of $102.50 when they believe the stock will sensibly rise nicely above $102.50.

OTM choices frequently experience larger percentage gains/losses than the ITM option. Since the OTM options have a very lower price tag, a tiny change in the price of theirs can change in big percentage returns as well as Volatility. For instance, it's very common to find out the cost of an OTM call option bounce from $ 0.10 to $ 0.15 during one trading working day, which is the same as a 50% price shift. The flip side is the fact that these alternatives can go against you quickly also, although the chance is restricted to the total amount spent on the option (assuming you're an opportunity customer rather than the option writer).

Selling and buying put Choices are leveraged investments that offer the possibility to come up with huge losses or gains over a brief period. The two actual types of options are the calls and the puts. Places are betting that stock goes down in cost with a particular period. Nevertheless, depending on when and how you purchase or even market a put option, you could be betting because of the stock going either up or even going bad. It is beneficial to consider precisely how options work and just how you may profit from purchasing or selling them.

Tips

If you market a put option, you're betting the importance of a stock will surge in the future. Nevertheless, whenever you purchase a put, this usually means you anticipate the valuation of the stock is going to fall by the date of selection expiry.

8.3 Exactly how Put Options Work

All options have a price and a month assigned to them. For instance, you may envision a put option labeled "IBM Dec 100." If you purchase the put option, you're purchasing the proper to "put" a hundred shares of IBM inventory to the customer of the option of yours at hundred dollars per share before the option expires on the final Friday of December. Consequently, your put option is going to rise in value when IBM stock sets after the purchase of yours. The cost of the option of yours is going to accelerate faster when IBM falls below the hundred dollars per share indicated by the put of yours, which is referred to as the strike or maybe exercise selling price. When the cost of IBM is above a hundred dollars a share by the final Friday of December, your put option is going to expire uselessly.

8.4 Just how Put Options Priced Are?

The price of an alternative may be split into two components, the time value and the intrinsic value. The intrinsic worth of an option is driven by the present worth of the underlying stock. Since put option is betting that stock goes down in value, places with strike charges above the present market cost of the underlying stock are deemed to be "in-the-money." For instance, in case you possess an IBM Dec hundred put as well as the stock is trading at ninety-five dollars, which put has an intrinsic worth of five dollars because you can purchase the inventory for ninety-five dollars per share and "put" it to somebody who needs to pay out hundred dollars a share.

The time value of an option is dwindling. For an option heads toward the expiration date of its, the time value of its is going to head toward zero.

Consequently, alternatives with lengthier terms have higher intrinsic worth. For instance, if IBM trades at ninety-five dollars per share in January, an IBM Dec hundred put is going to be well worth over an IBM Feb hundred put, since the choice comes with yet another ten weeks showing an income.

If you add in concert the intrinsic and precious time values of an alternative, you will receive the present market price of the feature.

8.5 Buying vs. Selling Put Options

Whenever you purchase a put option, you are creating a choice that a stock is going to trade lower before the option expires.

If you market a put option, you're making one of 2 various kinds of bets. The very first method to sell a put option is closing out a current position that you previously bought, at possibly a gain or a loss. For instance, in case you purchased an IBM Dec hundred put for four dollars per contract and also the price went up to nine dollars, you can sell your put choice as well as pocket the five dollars per contract gain.

Nevertheless, you can additionally promote a naked put. This means you are selling a put to not close out a current position you previously bought but only to open a fresh position. If perhaps you market a naked put, you're providing the customer of which place the proper to "put" the inventory for you in the strike price. For instance, in case you promote a naked IBM Dec hundred put, you might be pushed at any time to purchase IBM stock from a hundred dollars a share. Nevertheless, if IBM hardly ever trades under a hundred dollars before the December option of yours expires, you will not need to purchase the stock. You can just maintain the premium you got from the purchase of the possibility. Put simply, offering a naked put is the same thing as betting that a stock goes up, not done.

Chapter 9

Beginners common mistakes

Beginners' normal errors Option traders lessen obligations compared to regular inventory traders. As a novice in options trading, you must see how the duties of yours will differ in the capital industry. The most effective places to purchase stocks online won't enhance the experience of yours with options. When trading options, you're not needed to buy or even sell. Rather, you merely can exchange two kinds of stock options: puts as well as calls. The latest choice traders prefer you to become excited about the advantages alternative traders receive. Many folks allow their excitement to get the very best of them, and wind up losing much more than the profit. To be able to refrain yourself from associating with the unsuccessful, read on, and find out about the best novice option traders mistakes to stay away from.

Starting Too Big

The very first mistake most beginner options traders do beginning overly serious. Even though the expression "go big or even go home" might have been effective in favor of yours in days gone by, it won't do the job in the options trading industry. Start trading with smaller sized contract positions. The quantity of capital you spend is meaningless in case you don't understand what to do with it. By getting started small, you can get the hang of selection trading.

Next, when you've experienced that is enough to start selling far more contacts, you'll profit. Promote a few of shares at one time to begin the options trading journey of yours on the proper foot.

Utilizing Just only one Strategy

Yet another generally made a mistake most different options traders do use just one technique. Usually, options traders begin by trading short and long. While this Strategy might find you success, it shouldn't be the sole tactic you use. Investors who continue trading options the same way for long periods don't profit almost as people who implement an assortment of strategies. Options trading gives you numerous resourceful strategy options. You've much more potential techniques than you'd with stock trading. You can discover where you can invest in stocks relatively easily, learning how you can implement the proper choice trading techniques takes time. Do the homework of yours and then make use of the attainable techniques to the very best of the ability of yours. As a novice, begin with what is effective for you while concurrently studying brand new methods. Next, you are going to avoid this normal mistake new choice traders make.

Terrible Expiration Date Decision

The latest option traders likewise neglect to understand the strength of expiration. Although you've numerous options for the expiration date of yours, they're not all produced equally. To pick the best expiration date for you personally, you have to have an outlook initially. Base the expiration date of yours off of the outlook of yours. Think about just how long you believe that trade usually takes. Ponder whether you are going to profit much more by having the trade all through a stock split or perhaps not. Look at liquidity. To achieve success as a novice options trader, don't create a rash decision on the expiration date of yours.

Thinking Cheaper Is Better

Lots of beginner options traders drop out by buying out-of-the-money. In purchasing out-of-the-money, you're maintaining an option's premium cheap. A lot of the new investors choose this Strategy when they're advised not to go very big. Although you still shouldn't over-leverage, picking an out-of-the-money choice additionally doesn't present huge profits. Instead, such investments contained higher risks since they're less predictable. Less predictability can lead to surprising losses. Despite profile management's best practices, recording losses won't be an uplifting job. Aim to create smart options, not always inexpensive conclusions, when getting associated with selection trading.

Doubling Around Compensate for Losses

Lastly, refrain from doubling up to compensate for losses as an alternative trader. When investors like yourself start options trading, they wrestle with losing and leap into attempting to get up. They do so via doubling up to lower the per-contract cost basis of theirs. Although this can happen through doubling up, it generally doesn't. Rather, new options traders wind up compounding the risk of theirs. Instead of attempting to solve issues that have affected you and the capital of yours, close up unsuccessful trades. When you discover when you should close trades, you are taking a stride closer toward transforming from a novice options trader to a booming one.

As you go into the options trading market, you get numerous lucrative opportunities. Nevertheless, you can't take advantage of such possibilities until you understand the mistakes to stay away from. For starters, start little and then improve the number of shares you promote as you develop on the market. Teach yourself about the various approaches that some other investors profit off of. Take the period to plan out once the best expiration date is going to be for you. Realize that discounts may not be better. Finally, keep the head of yours on the shoulders of yours if you acquire a great deal of refrain and losses from doubling up to compensate for them. Today, you understand the way to stay away from the most typical mistakes beginner choice traders make.

Superior trading methods Techniques for options trading range from the easy with the complex - from fundamental one-legged trades to the four-legged monsters - but all techniques are derived from only two standard alternative types: calls and put. Each has downsides and upsides, and also you may wish to renew the Understanding of yours of what a call option is and just what a put option is.

Chapter 10

Advanced trading strategies

Below are five complex methods that develop from these fundamentals, using two options in the trade, or even what investors call "two-legged" trades. Generally, a brokerage can create these trades together with one transaction; therefore, investors do not need to get into each leg individually.

The techniques

1. The bull call spread

2. The bear pull spread

3. The very long straddle

4. The very long strangle

5. The synthetic long

The bull call spread

The bull call spread pairs much lower strike call with a quick higher strike call, each one with the very same expiration. It is a wager in which the basic stock is going to rise, but possibly not above the hit of the quite short put call. This trade caps the possible upside in return for higher percentage gains than buy a call. The long call protects the profile from the possible perils of the quite short phone call.

Example: XYZ stock trades at fifty dollars a share, along with a phone call in a $50 hit that can be obtained for $5 with expiration within six weeks. A $60 call that has the same expiration can be offered for $2. Here is the payoff profile of just one bull call spread.

Stock price at expiration	$50 long call profit	$60 short call profit	Bull call spread profit
$80	$2,500	-$1,800	$700
$70	$1,500	-$800	$700
$60	$500	$200	$700
$55	0$	$200	$200
$53	-$200	$200	$0

Stock price at expiration	$50 long call profit	$60 short call profit	Bull call spread profit
$50	-$500	$200	-$300
$40	-$500	$200	-$300
$30	-$500	$200	-$300
$20	-$500	$200	-$300

The stock price at expiration $50 very long call profit $60 brief call profit Bull call spread profit

Potential downside and upside:

The short call caps the possible benefit of this particular technique at $700, which happens during every stock cost above $60 a share. The profit comprises the $500 benefit on the very long call and also the $ 200 premium from the quite short phone call. The total price of the industry is $ 300, and that is the possible complete drawback in case the stock remains under $50 share.

Precisely why use it:

The bull call spread is a stylish method to bet on a stock's moderate cost rise. The bull call spread provides numerous advantages over only a long call:

• It costs much less to create (in this particular illustration, $300 versus $500)

• It reduces the breakeven point (from fifty-five dollars to $53)

• It reduces possible downside (from $500 to -$300)

• It offers a much better return as much as the short strike (a prospective 233 % return compared to 100 %)

The bear put spread

The bear put spread looks similar to the bull call spread, though it is a wager on the modest drop of a stock rather than an increase. The bear put dispersed pairs much higher strike put with a quick lower strike put. The method bets which the stock will fall, yet perhaps not very much below the lower strike selling price. This trade caps the possible upside in return for higher percentage gains than buying a put.

Example: XYZ stock trades at $55 share, along with a put in a $55 hit, can be obtained for $5 with an expiration within six weeks. A $40 put with the same expiration can be offered for $2. Here is the payoff profile of just one bear put spread.

Stock price at expiration	$50 long put profit	$40 short put profit	Bear put spread profit
$80	-$500	$200	-$300
$70	-$500	$200	-$300
$60	-$500	$200	-$300
$55	-$500	$200	-$300
$50	-$500	$200	-$300
$47	-$200	$200	$0
$45	$0	$200	$200
$40	$500	$200	$700
$30	$1,500	-$800	$700

Potential downside and upside:

The brief put caps this particular spread's potential benefit at $700, which occurs at every stock price under

$40 a share. The profit consists of the $500 benefit on the long put and also the $200 premium from offering the $40 call. The total price of the industry is $300, and that is the possible complete downside if the stock remains previously $50 at expiration.

Precisely why use it:

The bear put spread is a stylish method to bet holding a stock price tag is falling modestly. The bear put spread provides numerous advantages over only a long put:

• It costs much less to create (in this particular illustration, $300 versus $500)

• It raises the breakeven point (from forty-five dollars to $ 47)

- It reduces possible downside (from $500 to -$300)

- It offers a much better go back as much as the short strike (a prospective 233% return versus 100%)

The very long straddle

The long straddle pairs an at-the-money rather long call as well as an at-the-money lengthy put in the identical expiration as well as an identical hit selling price. The very long straddle wagers that the stock will move substantially higher or perhaps lower. However, the investor is uncertain in which direction.

Example: XYZ stock trades at $50 a share, along with a put and a call in a $50 strike are each out there for $5 with an expiration within six weeks. Here is the payoff profile of a single long straddle.

The stock price at expiration	$50 call profit	$50 put profit	Long straddle profit
$80	$2,500	-$500	$2,000

The stock price at expiration	$50 call profit	$50 put profit	Long straddle profit
$70	$1,500	-$500	$1,000
$60	$500	-$500	$0
$55	$0	-$500	-$500
$50	-$500	-$500	-$1,000
$45	-$500	$0	-$500
$40	-$500	$500	$0
$30	-$500	$1,500	$1,000

The stock price at expiration	$50 call profit	$50 put profit	Long straddle profit
$20	-$500	$2,500	$2,000

Potential downside and upside:

When the stock goes up, the possible benefit of the lengthy straddle is infinite, much less the price of the 1dolar1 1,000 in premiums. In case the stock declines, the possible benefit of the put choice is the complete value of the basic stock minus the price of the choices' premium (so $ 5,000 minus $1,000, and $ 4,000).

The possible drawback of the lengthy straddle is once the stock doesn't go very much, in the number from $40 to $60 share. The maximum downside happens at $50 share, with both choices expiring worthless.

Precisely why use it:

Given the large price of establishing a very long straddle, investors make use of the technique just whenever they are wanting a huge price campaign but do not understand which way the stock may run. In this particular illustration, the breakeven is 20% above or perhaps under the starting stock cost. That is a tremendous hurdle for establishing a very long straddle. However, that sort of move could occur in the industry, including biotechnology, the place that the release of crucial research results could whiplash a stock 50% or higher in one day.

The synthetic long

The synthetic night strategy pairs an extended call with a quick put at the same strike and expiration price. The intention is usually to imitate the upside functionality of truly owning the underlying stock.

For any synthetic long, the proceeds from promoting the put help counterbalance the price of the call, and often investors need to erect little or maybe no total investment. Much more ambitious synthetic longs could be put in place at a strike priced higher compared to the present stock price, while much more synthetic longs are set up beneath the stock price.

Example: XYZ stock trades at $50 share, along with a put and a call in a $50 hit are out there for five dollars with expiration within six weeks. Here is the payoff profile of a single synthetic long.

The stock price at expiration	$50 call profit	$50 put profit	Synthetic long profit
$80	$2,500	$500	$3,000
$70	$1,500	$500	$2,000
$60	$500	$500	$1,000

The stock price at expiration	$50 call profit	$50 put profit	Synthetic long profit
$55	$0	$500	$500
$50	-$500	$500	$0
$45	-$500	$0	-$500
$40	-$500	-$500	-$1,000
$30	-$500	-$1,500	-$2,000
$20	-$500	-$2,500	-$3,000

Potential downside and upside:

This payoff profile is like it'd if the investor had possessed the inventory directly. For instance, at a stock price of $80, the investor gets a total advantage of $3,000 with the stock along with the synthetic lengthy. And so, love the inventory, the possible benefit is uncapped, but just up until the option's expiration.

The drawback of the artificial lengthy occurs if the basic stock goes to zero dollars. Then the same as the quite short put approach, the investor will be made to purchase the inventory in the strike price and understand a complete loss. The optimum drawback is the complete worth of the underlying stock, here $ 5,000.

Precisely why use it:

The synthetic long could be a useful method to get the functionality of stock without committing any total capital. (That is infinite prospective returns.) In exchange, the investor should be prepared - and, significantly, equipped - to purchase the stock in case it declines beneath the strike price at expiration. Much more intense synthetic longs at a strike above the stock price may even lead to a total funds advantage on the account. That is a lot more attractive for bullish investors.

10.1 Conclusion

There's a large amount of info crammed into this particular book, all to try and enable you to be much better ready to trade stocks as well as specifically option making use of technical analysis. Trading is a procedure, and also like every procedure, the greater prepared you're, and the greater number of training you get, the much better you could be at it. This book began the guide with a quote from Seneca - "Luck is what goes on when planning meets opportunity" - and also has authored the chapters from that viewpoint. You need to be prepared to exchange, as well as be ready to make use of any success that the market provides you with. You today have a feeling of what it takes being ready, at minimum, to trade from a technical perspective.

We explored how you can determine the main pattern and what influences. This is crucial because seventy percent or more of all the stocks move together with the trend if you've received little else from this particular publication but an understanding of how you can determine the pattern as well as benefit by trading with it.

CPSIA information can be obtained
at www.ICGtesting.com
Printed in the USA
LVHW021359250421
685423LV00002B/41